PARSONAGE

A COUPLE HUNDRED PARAGRAPHS OF MADE-UP CONVERSATIONS

NISHKA M. DASH

Copyright © Nishka M. Dash
All Rights Reserved.

This book has been self-published with all reasonable efforts taken to make the material error-free by the author. No part of this book shall be used, reproduced in any manner whatsoever without written permission from the author, except in the case of brief quotations embodied in critical articles and reviews.

The Author of this book is solely responsible and liable for its content including but not limited to the views, representations, descriptions, statements, information, opinions and references ["Content"]. The Content of this book shall not constitute or be construed or deemed to reflect the opinion or expression of the Publisher or Editor. Neither the Publisher nor Editor endorse or approve the Content of this book or guarantee the reliability, accuracy or completeness of the Content published herein and do not make any representations or warranties of any kind, express or implied, including but not limited to the implied warranties of merchantability, fitness for a particular purpose. The Publisher and Editor shall not be liable whatsoever for any errors, omissions, whether such errors or omissions result from negligence, accident, or any other cause or claims for loss or damages of any kind, including without limitation, indirect or consequential loss or damage arising out of use, inability to use, or about the reliability, accuracy or sufficiency of the information contained in this book.

Made with ❤ on the Notion Press Platform
www.notionpress.com

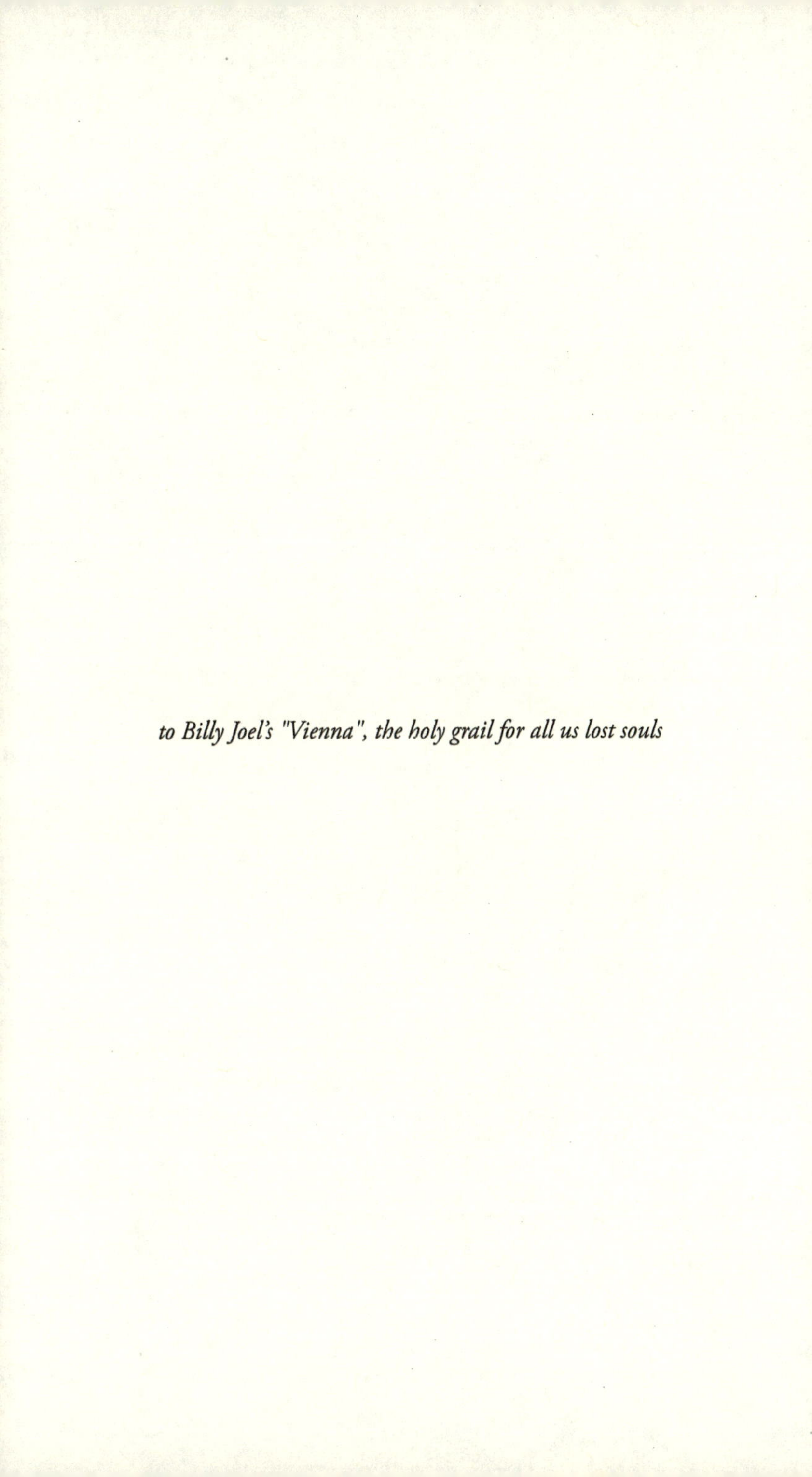

to Billy Joel's "Vienna", the holy grail for all us lost souls

Contents

Contents

Foreword

"For I have now become an unanswered letter, a poem without rhyme,
and ink that's been smudged and the cradle of the lost."
A somber self-reflection on mortality, femininity, and artistic despair.
I usually don't pick up poetry books but, I had to this time for Nishka. I've known her for quite some time now. When I met her the first time and even now, she stays to be this raw and open person who has always dwelled to view the reality in a much different perspective or if I may say as a more vivid and true perspective and this is truly what has been reflected in her poems. Feeling of being both alive and detached. It's the kind of writing

that lingers in the reader's mind, long after they've read it. There's something just so refreshing about this. The social commentary wrapped in mythological references, a love letter to an ordinary yet extraordinary person, nostalgia and that contrast between love and loss, warmth and winter. Every poem has its distinct voice and theme, each piece brimming with layered emotions and rich imagery. This book, this collection of poems, doesn't just emerge as any other but, the intimacy of these particular writings come forward as virtue of the truest human nature. Just like you being you, made me stick around this book too.

Love

Tiana

Preface

When thinking of the words to string together to write this preface, I wondered to myself (as I often find myself doing-mostly existentially) what is different in the words I string together and the ones AI does. Why do my words make someone cry or laugh, while AI stikes no such feeling? As a cessation to my never ending cycle of 3 AM thoughts, I came to the conclusion that AI is like us 21st century individuals- so engrossed in today's dilemmas that we forget to live and forget to learn that makes us devoid of feeling deeply, feeling truly.

The title of the book comes from a rustic villa named 'Parsonage' back from my first trip to Landour. The villa stood out to me as a contrast to the word itself. While the word indicates to clergy, luxury and facaded spirituality, the villa embodied the spirit of being mortal, discovery, transdental spiritual arena located in the midst of pines and oaks. The irony of this struck out to me days later while reading 'On Writing' by Stephen King that allowed me to delve into the very concept of discovering oneself and create a horizon between delusion, devoid and reality.Many books, movies, consellations, essays and songs later, here we are. Poetry mirrors the reflection of the villa named Parsonage, deep in the woods of Landour- A potrait of something different inside that contrasts sharply with its outward appearance.

This book is a collection of 30 poems spanning across the years 2023 and 2024 that gleefully plays with various mortal themes (especially grief over a lover) spanning over modern rennaissance, romanticism, existentialism etc. and one from back 2017, that could be construed as my first attempt to craft something from the writen word. We try to explore "Poetry" as a way of life rather than a literary technique that experiments with mixing the old with the new and plays with the uncertainity of the future in a metaphysical sense and how language is the driving force of the world, for if not for language the sciences could never have spoken. Additionally it contains certain side notes for some poetries and observational write ups crafted while sitting in a cafe rewriting people's converations, glares and more in my head along the poems to give the audience a general setting to embrace the poet within them. Many of these poems are highly metaphysical,and metaphorical and many share their names with grecian heroes that speak of unspoken stories. Many of these poems play with the concept of punctuation and own creation that fill the empty void of unspoken human emotions, a prodigal feeling.

The idea of this book had been concieved while feeling the intimacy of the written word that says what cannot be said, resolving one of the major challenges we face via the power of observation. The concept of this book had made me insecure for quite some while now as I feel this would act as an expose to the inner workings of my mind and make me vulnerable. However after days of contemplating the 'tommorow' ideology in life, I have concluded that we only live once, and wasting it on doubt, contemplation and questioning morality however fascinating it sounds leaves us void of the colours of life.If I could write this book once again I would probably add or remove a plethora of things, but as of now these few words will suffice. (probably remove it all except the cover page). With a heavy heart, I do think in penisive hours, that this book may not sell a lot, but it being out there makes me feel like Dorian Gray in my own way, a feeling that is hard to string within words. Before self publishing, I took rounds on sending this draft to several reputed publishing houses and faced several rejection letters with a nonchalant smile, so if you too are an aspiring writer, do not ever be crestfallen if your first draft doesn't make it, because eventually the pieces will fall together and make way for your masterpiece into reviving a dying art.

The exquisitely majestic cover designed by the coolest human being on Earth, Himani Rawat is not done justice with mere words. If anything can be classified as the optimum creative persona is the one that this cover holds. The pomegrenate seeds spilling out of the pomegrante symbolically are alike thoughts spilling out from the human shell as we proceed to converse with our inner self. "GMT 2017" signifies the period of time I spent in the city of spires that always holds a special place in my heart as being the prolegmenon of my writing journey and established in my brain that I could play with words and be a crafter of the written word. Once united, now a beautiful mess just like pomegrenate seeds!

Back when I read my first book Matilda, I fell in love with the concept of art. I still vividly remember leaving a voicenote to my self after rereading books leaving my imprint of my perception, with one saying, *"There is something about art, whether it be the written word, painting, music etc. that feels different, feels right and gives the assurance of the flesh and blood around us that can never be found through technology. Its there, its concrete, and no matter how far in the future we go, we will never be able to forget art, because we cannot uproot our roots...it why we are humans and not robots."*

ps: treat this book as your personal therapist by an eclectic grandma for those days we've all felt in this century :)

The best way to read this book would be to tuck a cup of coffee, a notepad and a pen, and this book in a bag and go outside to feel the sun and the living breathing figures around you. I know this book probably will be lost in the shadows of time but it being out there makes me feel immortal in a way, to pertain my filmy, old-school thought process out for the world to feel and see. Let us embrace the Sylvia Plath within us and with the rusting pages of this book mark the confluence of man and thought, whilst being 'on the road'.

Acknowledgements

When Phoebe Buffay said, " Boyfriends and Girlfriends are gonna come and go, but this, this is for life." I felt it. I've had a million aquaintaces in my life but a few people who have felt like warm scarf on a chilly winter morning. A few people who felt like home.

First and foremost, I dedicate this book to the my oxygen and water, my yin and yang, my dearest Mom and Dad. Thankyou for always believing in me regardless of life's response to me. Thankyou for the many inside jokes that never failed to make me laugh, that one last episode of Friends and bite of rasgulla, for always pushing me towards being and good person more than being a succesful one. Thankyou for that warm hug or comforting shoulder to shed those tears. Thankyou for being the greatest parents one could ever have, and with this book I make a pact to try and be the 'perfect' daughter you deserve. You once asked me, if I wanted to be like you or be greater person, and say it out loud- I wish to be like you two because you are the two greatest people one could ever meet.

Secondly, I dedicate this book to my purple, my mussorie in the form of person, the lane to my rory, my comfort zone and the one person I can be myself with regardless of the time; my best friend Tiana. Thankyou for being the greatest best friend a girl could ever have. Thankyou for always being my rock of support, when I was at my lowest. Thankyou for those comforting inside jokes, midnight conversations, gmeet calls to discuss everything under the sun.If not for your belief in me this book would've always been a couple of notes on my phone and in my diary. Thankyou for being the angel you are to guide me when I felt lost, and most importantly, thankyou for always being there. (PS. Next you need to write a book because that foreword made me cry). I wish we had met earlier, for life feels empty without your smile now!

To Himani, who made my dreams look better than I imagined. You're my forever partner-in-creative-crime. The Robin to my Ted—you are the kind of friend everyone dreams of having but only a few are lucky enough to find. Your art doesn't just sit on paper; it breathes, it feels, and it tells stories even I couldn't put into words. This cover? It's like Sylvia Plath and Phoebe Buffay teamed up in an alternate universe—it's haunting, poetic, and so unapologetically you. You've taken my messy, chaotic ideas and turned them into something so exquisite that words feel tiny in comparison. You're not just the illustrator of my book; you're the heartbeat of its soul. Thank you for being you—brilliant, creative, and the coolest human I know.

Next I want to thank my seniors Vrinda and Shwiti who I have always looked up to, Thankyou for being the most enthusiastic readers for whatever I write, being the bestest proofreaders and giving the sweetest acknowledgments that feel like the warmest of hugs on the coldest nights.

I wish to thank my teachers Ms. Ashwarya Priyadarshini for teaching the most of the little I know of Literature, being the one of the best proofreaders and for teaching me how to read like a writer. From signing my rec letters to being one of sweetest people, thankyou for it all. To Ms. Ruchika Makkar, thankyou for all your late nights advices, sweet comments on many of writeups that made me feel that I could be a crafter of the written word (PS. your sarcastic comments, philosophical discourses and jokes have never failed to make my day).

Thankyou Ekam, Tanush and Ruhaan for your encouraging conversations, Divit for always making me laugh and being the first one to put the idea ofwriting a book in my head, my seniors Ekansh Wadhwa and Suhani Saxena and my former teacher Venkatesh Sir who have knowing and unknowingly inspired me to unreachable depths, Zayan and Vaanya for always being the better writers who made me fall in love wih writing even more, Grandma and Grandpa for your blessings, Naisha for guiding me through the publishing part, Saiyasha for making the best cookies and Vikas sir for the most encouraging words. Thankyou to my fellow peers and family who have helped me shape this book into reality.

Last, but certainly not the least, I thank you dearest reader for picking this book up to find yourself from the confines of your armchair through the silly little paragraphs by a delusional 15-year old girl. I hope that my sidenotes helped you find the writer within you!

Love,

Nish

Prologue

"I can never read all the books I want; I can never be all the people I want and live all the lives I want. I can never train myself in all the skills I want. And why do I want? I want to live and feel all the shades, tones and variations of mental and physical experience possible in my life. And I am horribly limited."

Sylvia Plath

(ps: everything in life is writable, you just need the guts to write it)

1. Lord Almighty, Bless My Lover. (2017)

(Back in 2017, when I was rereading Dan Brown's Da Vinci Code, I felt intrigued by the underlying tones of distorted and haughty lover's redemption and romantic divinity. This particular piece is inspired by ths underlying theme and Cosimo's A Satyr Mourning Over A Nymph (after all us mortals are plagirised copy of one another). It depicts the scene of a lover's dilemma over seeking redemption for it's lover who is woefully being punished. Instead, the lover seeks self punishment and rebirth for its lover.)

lord almighty bless my lover,
for i kneel down to repent my sins,
it was i who drank the estilled wine from her lips,
and condemned her of sacrilegious cacophony.
curse me lord, for my blasphemous crimes,
but not my lover my lord,
for she's pure as fire,
intoxicating as wine,
sweet as the talin,
and for me the holy divine
it's not her you should deem your loathe upon,
but me my lord, your humble servant,
for i tresspased my boundaries,

and surrendered my virtue,
at the altar of desire.
for it's the flame we burn with, that cleanses our acts,
let that holy fire consume me, and let my flesh char with your cackle
For i am your servant, and you are my master.

2. Ink Scrolls of a Young Poet.

Beneath the veil of midnight's disdain,
A riddle of the soul, a cobble street,
Where footsteps echo, clandestine and coy
A mockingbird's laughter in the midnight fray.
A ghostly soliloquy, a twisted rebirth.
Midnight's requiem, an esquire infinity profound,
In the lurking quiet shadows, sits the silhouette of
A young poet, sitting with a quill dipped in ink
Wishing to the master she once did whim,
To see her scribbles once more
But alas the master must sigh
That the tale never ends
Life ebbs away but the ink cannot withend
With the final stroke of midnight
You enter a new page
The droplets don't show no more the glistening tears and blood
But a smile with no fears,
Sleep my sweet child as the holy said to thee,
let the celestial ballad softly play,
In the quiet theatre of shadows, lies the wilted ink scroll of a young poet.

3. Man behind the Pallid Veil

(If Kafka felt an ode to write a letter to Ms. Austen, giving a modern take of Elizabeth Bennet's view)

men leave vices, men leave virtues,
men leave dust as they whisk away, leaving a dawn in the wake
from our first breath, we are bound to count days until our last.
men who count days, die everyday.
fetch me a man, said lizzie bennet with the halo of fantasies hovering over her ribboned locks, and matched my wearily insouciant gaze.
fetch me man who counts days he lives and not the days till his last
fetch me a man, who drinks water like elixir,
eats food like ambrosia and pertains life as a symphony.
i say to lizzy bennet, no such man walked the earth,
who footsteps didnt burn the holy ground,
ask for the voiceless claim such a man breathes his last, everyday
its gluttonous how life consumes us all,
gnawing at the very pallid flesh of our bones,
like death knocking on our doors,
dressed as the man behind the pallid veil

the world has consumed us, has consumed us fresh
for lizzie you've stepped in a world not of blossoms, but one full of felled trees
for lizzie you've stepped into a graveyard, where haunts the ghoul of the man behind the pallid veil

4. Rye on Toast.

drafted windows, and cracked ceilings
I sit there, staring out.
seeing you fading out and standing in the rain,
drowned in the glory of bashful unawareness,
the cold droplets grazing your ebony hair were the saltine hot tears.
I watched you fade in once again and wept like a long-caged phoenix.
I felt the scarlet rush when your fingertips grazed my palm,
and wished to leave my skin, and waft into yours
Is it better to speak or to die?
I asked myself as I drowned myself in the miserable pools of my eyes,
I bent and rose and metamorphosed into a fallen ballerina behind the drapes.
I danced around,
gay, fresh and maroon
in your theatre,
Until you dropped my strings,
and I fell.
sunken beneath the cracks of my cherub cheeks,
I wake up now and force sunlight on my eyes,

as I see the butter sink in the bread and wonder why were we always rye on toast?
bread and butter as we may, find sanctity in the other's company,
the warm buttery melt grazes my toasty plain chin now and leaves a burning trail,
mocking my plain state,
for I am forever the stale old toast, lying on the counter,
weeping through my boring holes, while you being rye,
perch upon the top shelf, basking in your crystalline jouissance
blissfully oblivious as I try to reach for your hanging wreath,
and topple over to fall on the cold floor, strewn across my torment.
occasionally I drown my sorrows in the cans of detritus,
broken and fragmented, reveling of all I lost when I lost your gaze,
while you occasionally bathe in milk, who in her warm arms sways you around.
yet through loops of life, you find me on the same spot and I bask in the glory of seeing you from afar,
I lit candles and drank the wine, and play the memory of your ocean eyes in my head,
like a record player.
after all these years, I find myself on the same road once again,
and ask myself once again, is loving blinding yourself to the world?

is it better to speak or to die, and the poignant wrenching beheaded memory,
drifts back to me, like a wooden boat in the rocky waters
reminding myself that I died a thousand deaths when I spoke my heart away.
and as lie in my broken grave of the shattered holy grail, by my window side,
I smile softly in the honey light, at the thought of seeing you once more on the highway to zion.
I wish to return once more, as a little dandelion,
One you pick up in your soft paws, and blow upon,
and I weep once more, this time in the lover's emollition,
as I whisk away in your soft warm breath, to distant lands.
where I stay dressed in my white dress, cacophonic in my writer's euphoria,
drunk in heartbreak, from a stranger, I never knew but worshipped,
and that's why we are rye but never butter on toast, for butter sells its heart to one
and melts into them, while rye floats on the higher ground, waltzing around with milk,
oblivious to the damp bread it left on the stale ground.

5. Hope in Sunset Boulevard

i sat at the pier beyond sunset boulevard,
the sun melted and dripped like honey from sky's sword,
into the rippling waters.
it was melancholic scene, like a stage with a broken mime,
the humanly haze tied its legs down, and society blinded its eyes,
that's when i saw her.
hope bennington.
with ribbons in her hair, a pretty little frock down her knees,
with the summerset dandelions in her hands,
to ink her blue eyes, and her paint streaked little palms, is a blessing
her sweet innocence, her infectious little laugh.
the warm little breeze you felt as she blew the dandelion feathers away from the pier,
the sweet saltine caramel glazed lips.
the day hope allowed me to be reborn.
winters had passed, and autumns had withered away,
springs had bloomed around, with hope within its yard,
playing around with her little blue bicycle,
a forever frozen polaroid by sylvia plath, i wished.
but happiness, flew away like a butterfly.

i stood at the pier, and saw her house ablaze,
grief struck father and mother bennington,
as though the life had been wrenched out of their bodies.
the day the cursed summer turned the world black and white,
like a checkerboard, with no pieces,
so horrific yet so serene as her laugh rung out from the flames.
the day hope died.
years flew away, and i found myself standing at the same burnt and charred wall,
yellowed by time, and rubbled with hard years,
marred by the shattered kaleidoscope of the fallen butterfly's wings
the memoir of grief ever-frozen by the horrid sonnet that passed it by.
hope bennington- 1986-1993.
angelic daughter.
perhaps,
when we find ourselves wanting everything,
it is because we are dangerously close to wanting nothing.
read your tombstone, with wilted violets at its feet
the day you should've blown candles, the candles consumed your bones,
and i still find myself wandering around the dead garden, with the cinnamon scent of you,
and a dandelion feather passes me by, and i shatter once more with a frozen saltine grin
its funny.

we live as we die and we die as we live,
for life is a state , and i forbid you to ask what state i am in,
i cannot make you understand.
i cannot make anyone understand what is happening inside me.
i cannot even explain it to myself, said kafka.
and that's the sound i heard as i died a million years ago.
the day my hope died.

6. Palette of the Wilted.

The hues.
they melted from the sky to the earth, and dripped like honey from a child's mouth,
As we gazed at the stars
i hunched my tired shoulders
Weary from the insouciant human gaze
with cracks on my spines,
my face is sagged from the plastered smile I put up,
The reds of my cheeks have gone blue, and the hue of my eyes has stormed away
the roses claim they're wilted
the thorns claim they're in bloom
What can I say? The world is full of liars

7. Florentine Funeral.

saltine.
she smelt saltine, like wilted flowers,
that stand at the threshold,
of the muddy pool in your backyard,
with graceful water traces.
she bent over, like those lilies, ever so graceful, ever so melancholic.
she doesn't feel pain for she's like the ballerina's toes.
she smiles, as her veil envelopes her,
for her clock seems to be ticking yet her dial seems to have stopped.
she smiles silently as she looks in the mirror,as one solitary tear,
trickles down her face,
the fig tree, the sunlight bliss,
the ribbons in the hair, the joys of girlhood.
i think i forgot to be happy
for that girl is me and my ship's lost,
hush now, i'm not a poet,
but a coward at its best
the mirror cracks and so does my smile, for i have now become an unanswered letter, a poem without rhyme,
and ink that's been smudged and the cradle of the lost.

time has yellowed my pages now,
pourquoi-ai-je de crèe?
for my curls have flattened down , my rosy cheeks are sagged,
it's a flower funeral dear,for i'm a poet now
my corset strangles me and as i lay down with a solitary smile,
i am one with the world, yours truly, sylvia.

8. Religion.

You wear my skin,I'll wear yours
We'll go to that carousel
In that little sweet village
Wipe my ears, after that luminescent bath
Under those honey lights
Tuck me in bed, blow out the candles,
And kiss me goodbye
When my skin burns away,
It won't be mine anymore,
For I don't have a skin anymore,
It's yours
Your sweetness seeped in,
Leavaging the fire that consumes me,
That sugary scent is not me anymore,but you, three parts dead
with me
it's a rabbit hole we go down,
Except the hole is sealed off now,
Crystalline in time.
Lord let me bring her to my rite of time,
Let her lay beside me,
For without her I was not taught to love,
She's my mother, she's my lover,

She's my goddess and she's the mirror that loves me in my shriveled past
She's the mask I wear, let me kiss her portrait
For my being asunders in her worship

9. Best of Times, Worst of Times

(From the pen of Todd Anderson, Peter Parker, Remus Lupin and Elio Perlman)

in the morning light, i raced to the shore,
your voice in the air, lines you'd recite,
as i spoke of the stars, of poems, and night.
snowflakes like whispers fell soft on our skin,
in the warmth of the dawn,
under the searing sun of a winter's embrace,
i found solace in the contours of your face.
i drown in the echoes of a hypocrite's dream,
and breathe in the dust of what's left of us.
melancholic mornings, the snow starts to bleed,
under the silent sun, in this tragic ballet,
i'm left with the ghosts of the words i never could speak,
as that bullet rushed past your temple, and body dropped limp
i suffocate on the memories, wishing they were mine.
for you saw my scars, the darkness i hide,
now i'm lost in the echoes where i used to confide.
winter's embrace, a cold, bitter end,
to the warmth of the mornings where you were my friend.
now i wander the dock, with your name in my breath,

in the silence of sorrow, i welcome my death.
i cease to drown in the lake the poets went to die
for i'm crippled by your absence
you were my beacon in the darkened sky,
the truth in a world built on beautiful lies.
now i'm screaming your name to the void, to the sea,
without you, there's no more poetry in me.
dear achilles come down, put the intox down
for the poison runs in my veins
and there is no me without you

10. Flannel Shirt

i stood there in the rain,
flowers in my hand,
the flannel upturned against the wind,
and a satchel with your letters
you stood there against my door,
unable to knock unable to go,
with books in your hands
you took from my shelf before
has it been ages,
has it been decades,
since the dust settled against my door,
since the day you looked away and refrained
since the day that picture frame broke
who said i wasn't a romantic?
ofcourse i was
i pined for you, i burned for you
like those stars aeons afar
Oh the scars you gave me and then left me alone to die,
Oh on the fateful day you looked away and never turned back,
Oh how I despised you.
At last I felt so much
So I stopped feeling.

But I still preserve your flannel shirt akin to flowers pressed in books
And on the days you inhabit my slumber I wear it to cry my sorrows out.

11. Maneater.

Bloody teeth, gritty face
Smell of blood that lingers around.
satan's a romantic but a maneater
Eats boys for breakfast,
Girls with pigtails for lunch and pseudo men and women for dinner.
Her canines are sharp,
that pierce the flesh
Rip it, chew it, spit it
It's a cleansing ritual.
One day you may wake up,
To see that toothbrush alone.
all you have of your muse,
is the flecks of mint on the mirror.
Wipe them up real quick,
For she'll haunt you at night
Beware,
maneater ahead.

12. The Redemption of Apollo and Artemis.

In name of humanity, you strip us bare,
In the name of equality, you bleed our eyes raw till they thaw,
In the name of equity you steal our bounty,
In the name of pride, you burn our skin to embolise color
For social construct, you reign us hollow,
You tie our hands down, and burn us witches.
What have you done?
Conceived prescient humanity that rob us of mortality.
And rip us bare, maybe humanity was our biggest scam.
Wake up jesters of society,
Your house is on fire.
and it's all scampered .
scampering lies that suffocate us,
charring our souls and roasting our flesh,
taking in the joy of poetic cannibalism with every ring of the cackle,
the mad men, the fighters and the slaves all tie us down in the blessed sanctuary of Apollo,
While she sharpens her knives,
She, who is serene as the selene and darker than the night,
She who commands the stars, she who is the goddess of the night

She pierces our skin for we're fighting a battle we've already lost,
She adorns the pearls she pulls out from us,
For it's drenched in the sweat of innocent sin,
she lays our lips upon us,
And tastes like guilt.

13. The Beheaded Moth of Icurus

The ever glistening time frozen grimace and beautiful joy of a Polaroid
Captures everything in a blizzard of time
Ever so stirring ever so still
Like a moth drawn from the flame frozen in the resin and glass
With the dilated pupils and the wings all still
Like a mosaic of wonder through blinding light
There by the cobbled pavement, frozen still in time,
Lies the beheaded moth of icurus,
toppled from heavens above,
suspended by its cacophonic strings.

14. Fakir.

Anguish, agony and despair,
Midnights spent lying on the floor,
Covered in nothing but the stench of tears dripping off the eyes from sprinting a stream for anguish,
Cracked ankles with dried up blood,
From chasing death behind its swift wheels.
I lie down there, cold and numb.
I never felt pain of shedding tears
Before I saw maa.
Maa clinging on to the shell of what had been the skin of her child,
Covered with a white cloth, the child looked serene,
As if in deep slumber.
'Maa, why are you shedding such tears..he's just asleep'
Maa went frigid.
Her eyes had turned into a dried palette,
Her irises turned into watercolour,
And saltine strokes had cracked her cheeks.
'Oh, he is asleep. Asleep in a world with us mortals know nothing of. Wish I was asleep with him'
The child had passed on,
And with him had left his mother, leaving behind her damp kohl pallu in its wake.

Death had touched me that day,
Like a swan show,
Serene in its arrival, agnostic in its departure.
My gaze went off and saw another mother,
Unlike Maa, she wore a look of harsh acceptance, tinged with a haunting despair
Haggard look, disheveled hair,
Unlike Maa in her Benarasi pallu and Bareilly jhumkas,
The forlorn Maa sat on the floor, revelling in the acceptance of her young boy lying out cold,
He too wore the look of serenity, but his serenity looked burdened,
As if suffocating under the stifling debts the harsh reality lay upon his limp body
I never felt the complexity of being alone in the world,
Until I saw the forlorn young fakir's maa revel in the acceptance of losing her only hope of living,
Maa had bargained,
For her son couldn't leave in a world of luxuries, revelled in anguish and had now given up hope
While the fakir's maa, gently rocked her child's limp body,
As if gently caressing him to slumber with the jingle of her trembling chuddis,
The tremor of the glass chudis, and the clang of the glass bangles breaking,
Etched a thin, trembling line in motherhood,
Wearing the facade of society.

For we have it all in this world, yet live our lives stripped bare.
On nights like these,
When I'm still sitting on that white marbled floor, with stretchers rushing by,
I miss you, bhaiya
Yet I wish to have been that fakir's maa,
And see death in its purest form,
Unplagued by riches and raw.

15. Aphrodite.

I sat at the coffee shop,
sipping in my delusional sanctity,
draining the cup as hollow as my horror before,
I sat there, people watching,
In hope to strangle my misery as it conceived within me.
That's when I saw you.
Auburn locks, that swayed to the jazz,
sage eyes, cutting through hardest of storms,
honey tinged tan you wore as extravagantly as your wedding dress,
Aphrodite's fawned freckles strewed across,
Invoking jealousy from nymphs and angels heavens above.
To the ordinary eye, you looked like the girl next door,
But to me, with a laughter that felt like a warm scarf to the icy winter gaze,
You were the fireplace that melted the hungry iceberg within me,
you were in a sea of nymphs, an aphrodite.

16. Refuge.

Refuge.
In the stillness, whispers of ancient trees,
a solitary monk, in silent grace,
seeks the sacred refuge.
Breath by breath, the world unravels,
in the depths of trance,
where tides of peace silently swell.
heartbeat echoes the rubble on the hills
void of self, he absorbs it all
the fleeting joy, tender pain,
A lotus blooms in unseen depths,
where sorrow's shadow never lingers,
in this serene, enlightened state, as a solitary tear trickles down in devotion
heaven abode glimpsed in a moment.
the picturesque eyes, the cosmos, gleam,
threads of boundless life entwined.
a contrast to today's world of distorted, plastered smiles,
chained indulgences, lies humanity, a dead art,
where souls are chained to illusions, a bittersweet irony.
calmness but no mockery etched in the serene gaze.
In this tragic play, the monk finds peace,
a reminder of what is lost,

yet what still, in silence, can be found.
and as this powerful play goes on
you may contribute a verse. a petal. a thought.

17. Callisto.

(This partcular piece is inspired by Callisto's story. Callisto here is depicted as a young girl madly in love with another girl who she feels is way above her stance called Artemis who however has eyes for another man Orion. Callisto's love and devotion to Artemis is so rich that she accepts her fate of death when another man guised as Artemis wishes to love her. To express her devotion, she madly dances in love refusing to stop until Artemis looks at her with the same love(Not to invoke any religious blasphemy, but this story is also loosely based on the tales of Shyama, Meera and Radha and Medusa, Poseidon and Athena)(Theme- Joganiya))

I burned the midnight oil, smeared coal to brighten my eyes,
looked in the serene waters of the nyx ,fixed my sancted tresses,
To dance infront of you my beloved,
but you stand still, your smile ever so frozen in time.
release me from myself, for I have become yours
I am not me anymore, I am not of this world,
So I dance, and dance till my feet bleed, my hair shatters and my trinkets fall,
I keep dancing to please you, but you stand still.
Speak my beloved, my eyes have dried of tears but not devotion,

Speak, why don't you love me like him?

18. Cleopatra.

(inspired by the song "Cleopatra" by The Lumineers)
I was young once,

a starlet in the theater of dawn,

draped in whispers of silk and futures unwritten.

The world called me Cleopatra,

a name heavy as a crown,

its thorns pricking the soft flesh of my dreams.
The stage shifted, the curtains fell,

and the proposal of forever stood at my door,

a ring glinting like the blade of a guillotine.

I kissed its edges,

but turned away,

afraid to bleed.

Now I drive my chariot through the veins of the city,

seated in a throne of cracked leather.

Each passenger—a fleeting ghost—

sits beside me,

their lives a carousel of colors spinning too fast to touch.

I watch them slip away,

one after the other,

leaving echoes in the cab's thin air.
Regret sits heavy on my chest,

a stone warmed by the sun of my choices.

I wear it like an amulet,

both curse and talisman,

a reminder of the paths I carved with trembling hands.
I think of him,

the one who asked me to dance under a sky of stars

and call it eternity.

I was late—

late for love,

late for the wedding bells that never rang,

late for the life that could have been ours.
The roads stretch endlessly,

their gray ribbons unraveling into the horizon.

I am an actress still,

performing for the rearview mirror,

reciting lines of what-ifs and should-haves,

a soliloquy for no audience but time.
But even queens fade,

their reigns folded into history's quiet pages.

And I, too, will vanish—

my crown buried beneath the weight of silence,

my name whispered by the wind,

a ghost of a ghost.
Still, the meter ticks.

The wheels turn.

And I drive on,

through the corridors of memory,

through the labyrinth of my own making,

hoping to find a place

where the past might forgive me.

19. Take me to the Lake all the Poets went to Die.

Take me.

Take me to the lake where all poets went to die,

Take me to those serene waters where the voices of those writers lie,

to the banks where their pens took the eternal pause and where words faltered.

take me to the depths of the fated silence,

where their nightingale sonnets cry.
Take me.

take me to the hallowed halls of Rome.

where all thinkers took their last breath,

To the cerebral arches and boundless domes where philosophical prophecies lie.

take me to the burnt library, where those ink scrolls lie,

oblivious to the human eye.
Take me.

Take me to the broken astronomy towers,

to the cellular laboratories where our existential fate lies,

Take me to the truth, take me to the stars
Take me.

Take me to Westminster where all the greats lie,

Lying in the their heavenly beds in deep slumber,

Unaware of the cruelty as the day passes by.
Take me away,

Away to the land where humanity's wings lie shattered,

to the land where the writers, scientists, thinkers and poets have descended again

but leave me not alone, fellow pilgrim

for that holy land is not for my mere mortality,

For it is sacrilege to leave me amidst the divine,

for my sins pollute their waters,

My presence defies their lands and my breath hazes their skies,

Take me oh vagabond,

To the cottage above the hill,

With four walls and a window,

Where I may reside as a portrait,

residing in my solitude,

But my solitude won't be all consuming,

With the window that protects me from the crestfallen shackles of my human bondage and still let me see
the ubiquitous divine world.

Take me traveller,

Take me with the wind.

20. Wrong side of the Tracks.

(this particular poetry are slightly modified lyrics to a song I wrote back in 2023 I stumbled upon while spring cleaning my room, the wordings are slightly modified to give it a poetic jest. (this is was conieved while listening to Harry's house on repeat, especially Matilda, thankyou Harry Styles))

I was riding my bike, soaring on cloud nine,
daisies in bloom, and sniffling around lavender meadows,
dancing at midnight and baking cookies,
singing ballads like a bard from distant lands,
when my cloud burst, as I fell back to reality,
To the day I blew my birthday candles
and found myself on the wrong side of tracks.
the moonlight waltzes off my face,
as I give it a tired smile,
concealing it all behind till the smile runs out,
When did I forget myself,
When did I become sorry for growing old and moving somewhere without a reason,
When did I become afraid of growing old and being young at the same time?
I now stand in the midst of my old dusty room,

full of scrap and lumber of years tucked quietly in the back of my mind,
I bend down, and find a worn out diary,
tucked under floorboards, back from when I hid my life behind porcelein tiles and crazy fringe cuts,
and I break down seeing my little self, whom I lost in years to come with a piece of my heart,
"Its not a big deal little girl, that angelic smile hides it all" was my consolation in the middle of the nights,
The price I paid for fitting in,
It was the sign of times I never had.
" Dear Anyone willing to listen", I wrote
" I saw a girl today, beautiful as the sun and the gayest creature of them all, wish I was her and not her plagerized copy, cold and broken in its wake"
Wrote a little girl with hot tears dripping on the ink stained pages, which once again became drenched,
As those same tears flowed down the broken porcelein face, frozen in time of her future self,
And she sat there as the world passed her by,
In her little house, where lay hollow outcasts sheilded from never fitting in,
Sanctuary for those who never belonged, with a soft fireplace to dry the tears at the end of a weary day,
Of trying to belong.
And so the dust settles along the corners of the window panes,
Of the little white house, with little Matilda sitting within,

Still stuck in time like a record on repeat, and its a party,
For the ghosts of the haunting dust of outcasts,
Greeting pain like a long lost friend, the little house lies,
On the Wrong Side of Tracks.

21. In Between the Margins.

We were carved into each other's stories,

Ink-stained fingerprints on borrowed pages.

Your scribbles danced in the margins,

Half-laughed notes that tripped over words

Only you could twist into galaxies.

I found your heart in those annotations,

Each mark a glimpse of how you saw the world—

And how, impossibly, you saw me.
Do you remember?

The playlist of our lives was a single song,

Rewound until the tape frayed.

We laughed at the same misplaced rhymes,

Paused on the same haunting chords.

In those moments, you were a universe

And I was the astronaut, lost willingly.
We shared our chaos like it was sacred.

Your panic clawed at your throat,

And I held it back with trembling hands,

My heartbeat a metronome for your shattered one.

You said I felt like safety.

I said you felt like home.

And when the world dissolved into black holes,

We rebuilt it together,

One soft breath at a time.
But the story turned brittle.

Your sleep became fragile,

And I photographed the silences

As if the lens could hold you still.

Your laughter faded into the pages you left behind,

Margins empty,

Music muted.
And when you died,

The ink in my veins dried up too.

I read your annotations like scripture,

Searching for you between the words,

But every line I touched unraveled me.

Half of me was buried with you,

The rest of me wandered, like a vagabond.

I trace your handwriting

Like a prayer to a forgotten god.

The fabric a fragile mausoleum.

I replay our song,

But the rhythm is hollow

Without your laugh to catch the syncopation.
Love, they said, is eternal.

But they lied—

It dies a thousand deaths

When one lover is gone.

I am the afterimage of us,

Fading, fading, fading.
And yet,

The pages still hold your touch,

The margins still whisper your name.

I read your final note to me, scribbled in the margins of "Emma"

"Forever isn't long enough."

And even now,

I can't disagree.

22. Will a Pretty Face make it Better?

Dear future self, I write on a gloomy Tuesday night,
with a kettle burning on the kitchen top, flooded with bills alike,
take away menus and research papers strewn across the floor,
like mindless little cranes flocking the sea,
and the ink spills again, with the little burnt toast popping up,
and I leave behind my strewn papers, as an excuse to leave the soliloquy afar
They line up hearts like they line up faces,

a marketplace of symmetry,

eyes tracing the angles of my jaw,

never once meeting the curve of my words.
They've polished beauty into currency,

trading it like it won't tarnish,
I wish to speak through the dips of ink, that tie me down in my own little haven,
sitting in a little dusty room, with piled up junk and broken wine glasses

Each word, a fingerprint, smudged and intimate,

but who cares for fingerprints

when they only touch surfaces?
I write letters no one will read,

spill confessions like perfume on paper,

fold them into envelopes of aching honesty,

but the world wants gloss, not grief.
and so I sit down and ask, "Will a pretty face make it better?"

Better than the grace I stitched into sonnets?
I am a stranger in this cathedral of cheekbones,

a heretic who worships not at the altar of the airbrushed.

They look at me but never see me,

eyes grazing over words that are too heavy

for a world so light.
And yet, I keep writing.

Because when beauty fades,

Even if the world forgets my face,

they will find me in the margins,

in the pauses between lines,

in the ink stains of a life

too wild, too tender,

too real to be bottled or sold.
Will a pretty face make it better? I ask again
The crimson echoes in my broken flute,
No.

But a page, unpretty and raw, will.

23. The 22nd Bridge

(Backstory of this Poem- I recently had visited IHC and it brought back a the memory of sweet old times, where there used to be a little cozy place called Eatopia that I had visited times I've now lost count of, there used to be a science and art exhibition everytime we went, like a walk through gallery on astronomy or art or history or possibly anything under the sun, there used to be a beautiful art gallery with a beautiful painting of the view of a river from the riverbed and there used to be a large fountain with little orange and white koi. The memory became sweet and painful at the same time because nothing was same now, it had all been teared down. It was like losing a home)

The walls don't speak anymore,

not like they used to,
when whispers of bedtime stories

wove themselves into the cracks,
when laughter ricocheted off the peeling paint,

stubborn as the dreams

we carved into the wood.

The floorboards—

once groaning under the weight of small feet

dancing to songs no one else could hear—

now lie silent,
their creaks and sighs

a faint echo of the life they bore witness to.
Do you remember the window?
How it framed the summers—

endless skies and lemonade afternoons,
the winters, too, with their frosted sighs

and warm breaths fogging up

the glass we pressed our faces to,
imagining a world beyond

what we knew to be safe.
But now,

it is just a window,

watching the dust settle on a story

we were too young to understand.
How cruel it is,

to grow up and grow out

of something that once held

all the love we ever knew.
The house loved us back—

didn't it?
With every chipped tile,

every squeaky hinge,

every stubborn lock

that refused to let the world in.
It feels like the 22nd bridge—

the one that stretches into the nowhere fog,

its planks groaning beneath the weight of what-ifs.
Each step carries the echo of a door

that won't open again,

each breath a whisper of walls

that no longer hold your name.
You walk and walk,

but the end never comes—

just the void ahead,

just the emptiness behind.
The fog thickens,

swallowing the sky, the ground,

the smell of rain-soaked wood

that once meant home.
There is no lantern to guide you,

no voice calling you back,
only the haunting ache of a sanctuary

that was yours

until it wasn't.
And yet we left,

a suitcase packed with promises

to return someday.
But someday never comes,

and the house knows this.
It waits, still,

in its quiet decay,

like an old dog left at the roadside,

eyes fixed on the horizon

long after the car disappears.
How do you grieve something

that still stands,

its bones intact,

its heart broken?
How do you mourn a home

when the world calls it a house now,

when someone else hangs their coats

where your memories still linger?
And when you dream of it,

you are small again.
The air smells of rain

and mother's cooking.
The walls embrace you

like they always did,

like they still would

if only you could return.
But you can't.
You can't go back,

not to the warmth

of those four walls

that were once a universe.
And the grief of it—

of losing what was never supposed to be lost—

settles in your chest

like an heirloom

you never asked for

but can never throw away.
We went back once,

but it wasn't the same.
Someone else had painted over our childhood,

their laughter muffling our echoes,

their lives spilling into spaces

that still carried the scent of ours.
I ran my fingers over the banister,

expecting it to flinch—

but it just stood still,

like it didn't know me anymore.

My house was not a home anymore.
But as I left,

I swear I heard it whisper:
"I loved you anyway.
I loved you even when you didn't stay."

24. House of Cards

It wasn't the world that failed me,

it was my trembling hands,
the words that fell from my mouth

like shards of glass,
cutting through the trust we built

brick by fragile brick.
I stand in the wreckage,
a vandal of my own story,

the ink of regret bleeding

through every page I touch.
Your face—a constellation of disbelief—

haunts the sky of my sleepless nights,
and I keep tracing the stars,

looking for an apology

bright enough to rewrite the past.

I said I'd try.
But trying feels like running on quicksand,

like a vinyl stuck on the same lyric:

"I'm sorry, I'm sorry,"
spinning endlessly,

but never reaching the chorus of redemption.
Each step forward is a whisper,

a ghost of progress;
each step back—

a scream that tears through the marrow,

reminding me how easily

I betray the ones I love

and the stranger in the mirror.
I built a cage of my own guilt,
decorated it with the echoes

of words I should have said differently.
The walls close in like clenched fists,

tightening with every breath.
I try to claw my way out,

but the scratches on the surface

only mirror the scars inside.
I want to fix it,

but my hands are too stained

to sew the fabric of us back together.
Help me—please—
before I do it again,

before I watch myself

unravel the fragile threads

of every good intention,
before I become a ghost

that even I can't forgive.
I'm a sinner praying for chains,

a thief begging for his own arrest,

because I don't trust myself to stop.
Maybe I was always doomed to fall short,

a house of cards trembling

under the weight of expectations.
But still, I wish I could tell you—

I'm trying.
Not perfectly, not gracefully,

but with every broken piece of me

that still believes in the chance

to undo the harm,
to turn this endless record

into a song worth listening to.
Every word I utter is another bluff,
piling on top of this house of cards,
crumbling as I speak, like a sandcastle stuck in the hefty dunes.
And maybe that's enough.
Or maybe it never will be.
But dearest false lord, if you're listening,

I hope I'm better

in someone else's memory.

25. Unfinished Letters

(This particular poetry is about friendship, the one relation that trespasses the bounds of grief, hate etc. Thankyou Tani for being the muse for this poem, I know we all feel lonely at times, times we feel no one is our friend and we feel we are dying within, remember if you feel no one is your friend, you can atleast have this delusional 15 year old and the stars to cry to!)

There is a place where laughter echoes long after silence,

where sunlight lingers soft on the edges of memory.

Here, two shadows once danced—

carefree, like paper boats on a swelling tide.

Their hands, once tethered by invisible strings,

held not just each other,

but the weight of every secret, every wound

the world dared not see.
In the corner of their shared universe,

dreams were planted like wildflowers.

One whispered, "Do you think the stars ever get lonely?"

The other smiled, tracing galaxies

in the space between them:

"No. They have us now."
But time is cruel in its quiet unraveling,

a thief in the guise of days that stretch too far.

And one morning, the laughter stopped

like a bird mid-flight,

leaving the other to wonder

if the echoes were ever real.
A chair across the room sits empty.

The spaces between words grow sharp.

No hand reaches out anymore,

no stars are drawn.

Only shadows remain—

echoes of what was,

and what will never be again.
Grief wears many masks:

an unfinished playlist,

a half-written letter,

a name that burns the throat

when spoken aloud.
Still, there is a place inside where they live—

a garden untended yet still alive,

filled with wildflowers

that never learned to die.
And in the quiet, beneath the ache,

a voice lingers, soft as breath:

"Do you think the stars ever get lonely?"

"No. They have us now. Forever."

26. The Fire and the Tides

(Inspired by themes from Tennyson's Ulysses and the duality of duty and passion, a dilemma represented via a person trying to choose between artemis representing science and service and apollo representing passion and poetry- to feel happy by making the world happy or just be happy for being happy's sake)
Between the pull of tides and the burn of flames,

I stand—a fragile vessel of yearning,

Cradled by the moon's silver palms,

Scorched by the sun's golden embrace.

Two voices call, ancient and relentless:

One speaks of duty, of quiet labors beneath the stars,

Healing wounds unseen, mending what is broken,

A vow to cradle the aching world.

The other sings of fire, of canvas kissed by light,

Of words that burn and music that howls—

A dream too wild to tame.
I am torn.

The earth beneath me splits, a jagged crack,
A chasm of indecision,

Where shadows of my doubt dance like ghosts.

To heal or to create,

To mend or to set aflame—

Is there a path that bears both footprints?
I feel the moon weep through my veins,

Her light spilling into the void of my chest,

Soft and cool, a balm for my despair.

"Walk with me," she whispers,

"Gather the fallen stars and bind them to the wounded sky."

Her plea trembles like leaves in twilight.
But the sun, unyielding, rises in my soul,

Blinding me with fire.

His voice is thunder in my ears:

"Burn brighter than the worlds you seek to save.

Create, and they will know life beyond breath—

An immortality of beauty, carved in light."

His roar consumes the whispers,

And I am left in silence.
I cry to the void, my voice a broken hymn:

How does one choose between the heart and the hand,

Between love that gives and love that makes?

To serve or to soar—

Which will leave the soul unshattered?

Do I leave the moon behind,

Her arms empty of my devotion,

Or let the sun fade,

His blaze dimmed by the shadows of neglect?
The answer never comes.

The tides rise; the fire burns.

And I remain, a fleeting eclipse,

Caught between the sun and moon,

Praying to be whole

In the ruin of their light,
Too afraid to leave my wilted corpse in its wake.

27. Shades I Never Could Wear

The sky never learns to be the ocean,

no matter how blue it tries to become.

And I—standing in this field of hues—

am the color that doesn't belong.
I watch the reds of others burn,

fiery, proud, and certain.

But I am a faded rust,

hiding behind curtains,

pretending I am the sun.
The violets bloom in confidence,

a royal procession of purpose,

while I stumble as the dull grey

smudged between their petals,

too muted to be called alive.
The yellows dance in their brilliance,

a feverish joy I've never worn.

I stand in mustard shadows,

their golden glow always just out of reach,

their light exposing every flaw I bear.
How do you explain

that the green of envy does not sprout roots?

It lingers—untamed, hollow, bitter—

watching those who grow,

while I remain a barren canvas.
Even the blues I once trusted—

their melancholy soft as a hymn—

have become sharp and cold,

cutting into my chest as I wonder

if sadness is all I've ever deserved.
Each color, radiant in its own way,

spills over into the world,

but I am a spectrum-less void,

the absence of light,

a shadow pretending to cast warmth.
No color will bleed into me,

no red into purple,

no green into gold.

I am a palette of shades that never blend,

always pretending to be something more.
So I stand in this kaleidoscope

of other people's truths,

their pigments swirling around me,

each one a reminder

of how I will never be enough

to fill the canvas.
And still, the sky never learns to be the ocean,

no matter how blue it tries to become.

And I—nothing but a smudge in its vast expanse—

am left wondering

if I was ever meant to hold a color at all.
And I—nothing but a smudge in its vast expanse—

am left wondering

if even the void would weep for me when I'm gone.

28. Found Family (modified ballad)

Once there was a feather,

torn from the heavens,

adrift in the wind's cruel mercy,

its whispers lonely,

its flight aimless.
Once there was a flame,

flickering in the hollow of cold earth,

a prisoner to shadows,

its warmth untethered,

its light unseen.
They found each other,

not in grandeur, but in quiet cracks—

a feather caught in amber glow,

a flame fed by gentle breeze,

and in their meeting, the void lessened.
They built a world from scattered fragments—

a hymn in the silence,

a warmth in the frost,

a home in the wilderness,

where broken wings could rest.
But the world is a thief,

its hands greedy, its gaze cruel.

The flame dimmed beneath its weight,

the feather singed,

and the home began to wither.
Still, they clung,

a fragile union defying the void,

until the flame whispered,

"Go, before my ashes touch you,"

and the feather pleaded,

"But what is flight without your glow?"
The flame died with a crackle,

a laugh that tasted of sorrow,

and the feather was cast to the winds again,

its edges burned, its song muted.
Yet in every gust,

a spark lingers—

a warmth,

a memory,

a promise.
And now, the feather flies,

not alone,

but with the shadow of a flame

etched into its fibers,

guiding its aimless drift toward the sun.
The last light whispered not goodbye,

but this:

"Even in the ashes, you will find me,

for I was never the fire—

I was the warmth beneath your wings,
the found famiy you always wished"

29. Gray Walls

(seeing the heightening of rape crimes in my home country, this poem is written on the perspective of a mother who lost her only daughter to being a rape victim, this is the mother's plight and agony as the world tries to fakely sympathize with her for 4 days instead of taking any action and then its back to business, this poetry also is a reflection of how captial can be the silencing tape over an evocative cause)

The gray old buildings weep with me,

their veins of seepage like my own,

cracks splitting through plastered facades,

exposing the rot beneath.

They stand still, hollow sentinels,

watching a world that pretends to mourn.
Her laughter was once sunlight,

spilling through my ribs,

warming the marrow of my being.

Now, the sun is a stranger,

its light cruel,

its warmth foreign.
They came, with their bouquets of words,

dripping pity like leaky faucets,

each droplet eroding my resolve.

For four days, they stood,

their shadows cast long

against my shattered doorway.

And then, silence.

The kind that smothers.
The cracks in these walls deepen,

mirroring the fissures in my chest.

I cannot plaster over what is gone—

the echo of her voice is the wind

that seeps through the gaps.
They've returned to their noisy lives,

their clocks ticking in rhythm,

unbroken.

But I am left here,

a monument to ruin,

while the world builds itself anew.
The cracks spread,

and still, no one sees.

30. The Ashes We Became

(Upon reading Geetanjali Shree's Tomb of Sand, I was highly intrigued by how borders, partitions and divisions separate us from the very essence of living and make us hollow creatures with hazed breaths and dead grey matters and tired hearts. This particular piece is written as a long lost cry of a friend at the dead body of her other friend whom she was seperatted via the partition and was not even allowed to meet her before her death.)
They tore the earth like flesh,

their lines bleeding through rivers and veins.

We stood on either side,

hands outstretched,

fingers brushing the air,

the silence bruising our palms.
Your laughter, once a monsoon,

now a faint drizzle in my memory,

whispers of the rain that no longer falls.

My letters crumbled at the border,

the ink choking on soil

it could not cross.
Time, they said, would heal—

but it only carved absence

into the hollows of our souls.

Your name, a prayer unsent.

Your face, a lantern I cannot light.
When the news came,

it was not your death that shattered me—

it was my breathless impotence.

No flowers could bridge the divide,

no song could leap the chasm.

Only the wind carried my mourning,

and even she faltered.
Now, I am a husk

of unfinished goodbyes,

a shadow of a friend

who once believed the world was whole.

But we, the divided,

became echoes in empty rooms,

haunted by the fragments

of what could have been.
Tell me—

what kind of life is this,

when we are buried in borders

long before our time?

Note Of Gratitude.

Dear Reader,

As you turn the last page, I find myself humbled and grateful for the journey we've taken together—through ink and rhythm, across the landscapes of thought, emotion, and memory. These poems, though each unique, share one thread in common: they were born from the quiet spaces where the heart meets the mind, and where the soul dares to whisper its truths.

I cannot thank you enough for allowing these words to live in your hands, for opening yourself to the emotions they carry. A poem, after all, is not truly complete until it is read, understood, and felt. And in that moment of connection, the words transcend their paper prison and become something shared, something lived.

In this anthology, you've walked through moments of joy, sorrow, nostalgia, and introspection—much like life itself. Through each verse, you may have found fragments of yourself, or glimpses of others, but above all, I hope you found something that spoke to you, even if only for a fleeting moment with the touch of a little Patti Smith, and little Murakami and more

Thank you for being a part of this creative journey. For without you, the poems would have remained silent, echoing only in my own mind. It is you, the reader, who breathes life into these words.

May you continue to seek beauty in the quiet moments, to find depth in the simplest things, and to always remember that poetry is not just a collection of verses, but a bridge between hearts.

May this collection remind you that even in the vastness of this world,the art of observational writing, how to be a pure child of apollo and how there is always room for tenderness, for beauty, and for a moment's pause. And may it inspire you to pen your own verses, to share your own truths, and to continue seeking the poetry hidden in life's everyday rhythms. Afterall, without language and science and all philosophies falter, for language is the guiding beacon.

I'm always looking forward to reading and recieving your own verses and your take on the little paragraphs (especially those filled with critical commentry) I've presented henceforth. I can be reached at dash.niska1704@gmail.com via mail, or you can dm me on instagram at @nishka.dm1704 for a friendly greeting or a cup of coffee via gmeet with a child of apollo and pure connie baby stan! To check out more content by me check out my blog: michellestypewriter17.wordpress.com

With all my gratitude,

Nish

About The Illustrator

*"Feelings of mortal are so amaranthine yet so mercurial""people's dreams... have no ends"*Himani Rawat is a 15 year old highschool student, studying alongside Nishka, whilst being one of her closest friends. Her spirit animal is a hamster, who are known to be born with charm, humour and sweetness down to their paws, just like Himani. She is a talented illustrator, graphic designer and

photographer. Designing is something she has always aimed for. She happily devotes her time to, people who love to spend time with her and shakira ofcourse!

About The Author

"Where does it all lead? What will become of us? These were our young questions, and young answers were revealed. It leads to each other. We become ourselves."

— *Patti Smith*Nishka Dash is a 15 year-old highschool student who loves to read and write with every bone in her body. She lives in highly delusional Murakamiesque flimsy, currently brainstorming for her future book. She wishes to be an astrophysicist and scientific writer/ journalist in future. Her spirit animal is a cat, who are known to be observant, intuitive, creatively wise like her. In her free time, she can be found bingewatching cinema is all its evolving forms, occasionally sketching, screaming and playing piano to Arctic Monkeys on top of her lungs, and trying (sometimes failing) to be an overachiever to learn it all! She believes that if she had a cat size life she would backpack across the world and capture all its essence through photographic writing!

www.ingramcontent.com/pod-product-compliance
Lightning Source LLC
LaVergne TN
LVHW041117150826
845673LV00007B/2093

* 9 7 9 8 8 9 6 3 2 2 8 5 6 *